Crazy Bones

The Tale of a Waggy Tail
Second Edition

Lynne Wissink-Tressler

International Standard Book Number 13: 978-0-578-20886-2
International Standard Book Number 10: 0-578-20886-5
Library of Congress Control Number: 2019931285

BluewaterPress LLC
52 Tuscan Way Ste 202-309
Saint Augustine FL 32092
Printed in the USA

This book may be purchased online at -
www.bluewaterpress.com

Front cover design by Sydney Martin
Back cover photo by Milissa Sprecher Photography

Please note that address information is subject to change. At the time of printing, the address was correct, but may have changed since. Please check our website for the latest address information for BluewaterPress LLC.

Crazy Bones

The Tale of a Waggy Tail

Second Edition

Contents

About This Tale
(Explained by the Waggy Tail)

Everyone has a story, and ours is a simple one. It's about an ordinary woman in northern New England who takes in a feisty, extraordinary dog (that would be me), rescued from the streets of New Orleans following Hurricane Katrina. Our two personalities and how we see the world around us are very different. She thinks she rescued me, but I know better. Our tale is about our adventures, how we figured each other out, what I taught her about life, and of course, my very expressive waggy tail.

Dedication

This story is dedicated to three special groups of people:

First, there are those who take in animals and give them a second chance. The Cocheco Valley Humane Society in Dover, New Hampshire, is one such organization.

Second, following Hurricane Katrina, many airlines, crews, and flight attendants donated time and money to deliver abandoned animals to safer locations around the country.

Finally, dozens of nameless volunteers drove hundreds of miles and spent countless hours working as part of a huge relay network to deliver rescued animals from emergency shelters in the South to new homes across the country. Without their generous and loving efforts, many animals would not have had the good fortune of having a second start in life. They are heroes.

Thank you to all of you for your efforts in saving as many lives as you could.

Lynne Wissink-Tressler, PhD

Acknowledgments

The author(s) wish to thank many of the people whose support helped make this effort possible and who provided love and a watchful eye over both of us:

The Crays, Ruth and Walter Kurzenberger, Ernie Tressler, Jimmy Andrews, Kim and Jimmy Lyndes, Kelly Zuchowski, Lynn Willis, Tina Mitchell, Monica Chandler, the Murrays, the Faustinos, Eric Borrin, Dr. Tom Grebouski, Cousin Karl Palmer, Cousin Carol Palmer, and the McEneaneys.

Those who have treated and lovingly cared for Cray-Kur include the staff at Dover Veterinary Hospital in Dover, New Hampshire; Old Dominion Animal Hospital in McLean, Virginia; and Tails-A-Waggin in Fort Myers, Florida.

Thanks go to Jennifer McLean and Cathy Carroll for reading early versions of the manuscript and providing constructive feedback; Stacey Kimbell, for her help with local marketing; Dr. Robin Buckley, for pushing me across the finish line; Senior Production Editor Robin O'Dell and the editorial staff at Kirkus Media LLC for their collective editing skills; and finally to all my students, past and present, who have taught me so much and who continue to inspire me.

Thank you for the fun and crazy journey we've had!

Chapter 1

My Big Personality

It was *not* all about me, and I'm uncomfortable when anything is about me. I was a surly, middle-aged, reticent New Englander with a broken heart, but I was scrappy enough to push past "poor me" to restart life on my own. We Northerners are like that. There's no time for emotional nonsense when more important things need to be done . . . things like splitting, stacking, and bringing in firewood for the stove and filling Mason jars with the summer's harvest for sustenance during the long winters. The weather largely dictates the rhythm of life in northern New England.

My belongings and furniture were unpacked, and I felt settled in my new home on a short, dead-end street in a rural seacoast community on the Maine–New Hampshire border. I was delighted that I had found nearly everything I'd wanted in a home—a garage, tons of sunlight, a nice deck, privacy, and a few kind neighbors. It was good to be starting my life over. Life throws us choices, and I had chosen to move forward and forget about my broken heart. Besides, the whole concept of love had become a mystery to me and seemed to be an unnecessary distraction from the business of life.

Rebuilding my life exactly the way I wanted it was a dream come true, and not having to answer to anyone made it that much better. I could do everything my way, so I treated myself to a new TV, a workout machine, and new appliances. I was in charge of me.

But there was one thing missing: a dog. My own dog. I wanted a faithful companion that would cuddle up next to me when I read the paper. It had to be able to run as far as I could. It had to be smart and easy to train, affectionate, independent, clean, and easy to care for. Finally, it had to be a Hurricane Katrina refugee whose owner(s) could not be located. I wanted to do my part in giving an abandoned dog a second chance. I was so ready. I even had a name for it.

Now all I needed was the dog.

I'd read about all the animals abandoned by their owners after Katrina. Dogs, cats, ferrets, gerbils, horses, birds . . . all kinds of animals. Some could not be rescued when helicopters plucked their owners from rooftops. Some had become so malnourished or sick they had to be put down. I saw so many photos, and I knew I could help in some small way. Unfortunately, I would be limited to one dog because of the size of my new home and my work schedule.

Adopted dogs make great pets, perhaps because they know they're chosen. I didn't need a dog to dress up for Halloween and show off as a novelty to my friends. I didn't want a purebred or a high-maintenance dog that needed to be groomed every four weeks. I was fully capable and experienced at giving dogs baths.

It was a rainy September afternoon in 2005, just a few weeks after Hurricane

Katrina, when I made the call that changed my life.

"What kind of dog are you looking for?" asked Sandy, a volunteer who answered the phone at the Humane Society. It was the first of many questions that helped determine if I qualified as an adoptive parent. I couldn't imagine not qualifying, but I suppose some people who think puppies are little and cute and will always be little and cute, and who forget (or ignore) the fact that they require attention, training, proper exercise and nutrition, vaccinations, and physical exams. And that they get bigger.

"Have you ever owned a dog before? How many dogs? Where are they now? Who provided medical treatment for your previous dogs? What kind of home do you have? Who lives there? Do you smoke? Who will feed and exercise the dog? Are there other pets currently in your home? Why do you want a dog? What kind of dog or size dog did you have in mind?"

Her questions were fair and reasonable, and I answered them honestly, but at one point, I came dangerously close to disclosing that I was recovering from a broken heart and feeling lonely. I'd managed to stuff those feelings into a distant part of me, and I didn't want to be told that I might not qualify until I've had five years of psychotherapy.

"I want a young dog that is smart, lovable, and very athletic. It must be a dog that can run miles and miles with me. Oh, and it must be a refugee from Hurricane Katrina." I couldn't leave out that part!

"We always do our best to match dogs and owners, but we can't guarantee anything," Sandy said.

We talked at length about the dogs I'd had. Maybe that was my therapeutic moment. I guess folks who work with animals have a good understanding of people, too.

Sandy told me that volunteers had taken many dogs from New Orleans after Hurricane Katrina and driven them in a relay team to transport the dogs to parts of the country where they could be given new homes. Major airlines that had offered the use of their planes and were operated by pilots and attendants who had volunteered their time had helped transport other dogs.

"Your timing is pretty good, actually. We have a staff meeting Monday because there are new dogs scheduled to come in. I can share your request with the team and get back to you soon."

"Are these dogs usually pretty healthy?" I asked. "I have a big heart, but I don't want to adopt a dog with major health issues. I wouldn't be able to afford high medical bills." It sounded selfish, but I needed to be honest.

"All the animals we take in are not necessarily fit for adoption, but we have excellent veterinary resources, and we do our best to take care of all our creatures. The adoption papers come with a statement that the animals have been cleared by one of the vets. I promise I will call you Monday or Tuesday."

"Wow, that's great. Thanks!" I was already getting excited.

I hung up. *Yikes! I'd better get busy.* There was so much to do. I had to buy food bowls and a doggy bed. I decided not to tell anyone right away about the possibility of an upcoming animal adoption. I wanted to be sure it would work out before I made a big announcement. I credit (or blame) my German heritage with the need to plan everything. So Teutonic. So me.

When the phone rang a few days later, I looked at the caller ID and felt my heart beat faster.

"Hello?"

"Hi, Elizabeth, it's Melissa, the manager at the shelter. We had a staff meeting, and the team thinks we've got a good match for you. The dog's name is Jersey. She's a Katrina dog, and she has been cleared by the vet for adoption."

This was becoming real.

"Elizabeth, are you there?"

I couldn't believe my ears. They had a match. They had my dog!

"Yes, I'm sorry, I'm here. That's great news! May I come up tomorrow afternoon?"

"That would be fine," Melissa answered.

"Thank you so much!"

The next day, it was raining so hard I could barely see my backyard. What had been a grassy knoll was now an island in a pond that hadn't existed until now. Autumn had been miserable, cold, and wet, but the forecasters on WMUR said the nasty weather would be ending soon. Thank goodness, because a rainy fall in New England made all the beautifully colored leaves come down quickly. They covered sidewalks and roads and stuck to the car's windshield, making it hard to see, let alone drive. But foul weather would not stop me from my mission. The time had come, and I was going to get my new doggy, the missing piece in my life.

I had left work early to go home and change so I could get to the shelter before dusk. It gets dark early in northern New England. Jittery with anticipation, I put on my yellow raincoat and L.L.Bean muck boots.

As I eased out of the garage, I flinched as the rain noisily beat against my car. Slowly, I drove up the partially flooded main avenue through town toward the county buildings where the animal shelter was located. Many roads were now closed because of flooding, so I felt relieved that I could still use the most direct route.

I turned onto a dirt road that led back and forth up a hill, past the nursing home, the courthouse and jail, and eventually to the animal shelter. I should say it *had* been a dirt road, for the stones and rocks had washed away, leaving a path of muddy, deep potholes. There were huge puddles everywhere disguising the enormous ruts beneath them. I tried to stay on what I thought was the road. *Maybe I should have waited a day or two before making this trip. I don't want to get stuck in this mud.*

But there I was, ready to meet my dog.

I parked as close to the building as possible, zipped up my rain gear, took a deep breath, and pushed open the car door against the wind. I ran as quickly as I could, dodging puddles and trying not to slip in the mud.

I wasn't at all prepared for what happened next. I pulled open the door to the old clapboard building, unzipping my raincoat as I made my way through the feline section to the canine side. I looked from side to side at the rows of dogs in kennels. A dozen or so watched me. It was heartbreaking. They watched me so closely, pleading with their eyes: "Take me! Take me!" I wanted to shout, "Okay, everybody in the Volvo. Let's go!" I wanted to rescue all of them.

I had become so distracted looking in the cages that I'd forgotten why I was there. I was brought back to reality by a voice asking, "Can I help you?"

I jumped. "Oh my goodness. You startled me. I'm sorry. Yes, my name is Elizabeth. You called to tell me you have a Katrina refugee for me, and I'm here to meet her."

"Oh, yes! Hi, I'm Sandy. We spoke on the phone. We matched you with Jersey, a real cutie. Lots of energy and personality. We just got her. Let me bring her out." With that, she turned and went into a back room.

I started to smile in anticipation. My life would soon be complete. I couldn't wait to meet Jersey. I already had another name for her, but for now, she was Jersey.

When Sandy returned from the back room, she carried a small dog in her arms. My heart sank. *No!* I thought. I wanted a *real* dog, not a dog that couldn't possibly weigh more than fifteen pounds and couldn't keep up with me. How on earth could she run more than twenty feet? And she had these spindly little legs.

"I'm not sure she can run with me," I said, trying to hide my disappointment and decide if I should just say, *No, this won't work*. This jet-black doggy was compact and unique looking, but since I'd had only larger dogs, I didn't know what to think and just stood there, staring at her.

Sandy must have been reading my mind. These folks seemed to be good at that. She smiled and assured me, "Yes, she is only sixteen pounds, but she was bred to chase rodents. She's a Schipperke mix."

"A what?"

"A Schipperke. She has a bit of terrier in her, so she doesn't have the distinctive curled tail of a purebred Schipperke. Believe me, she is a runner! We've seen her run in the kennel outside, and she has endless energy. Why don't you take her home for a night or two? Get to know her. I think you'll see what I mean."

By now, Jersey was staring at me, as if sizing me up to see if I met *her* criteria as a prospective owner. I knew that dogs were smart and could sense things about people. Was I that transparent? Probably.

Um, people. Hello? I'm right here, and I hear every word you are saying. How about a little attention?

I felt a bit reluctant, but here I was, so I agreed to take her for a few days and "test drive" her in the morning when, I hoped, it wasn't raining. She was different looking, and that appealed to me.

Sandy gave me a crate to set up in my car (why hadn't I thought of that?) and a small bag of dog food (how did I forget *that?*). The people at the shelter amazed me because they operated on a sliver of money from the county budget and relied on donations of food, supplies, and money. Yet, they supplied me (and others, I presume) with some of the basics I had overlooked. They were clearly dedicated to the animals they took in and for which they provided care and medical services.

Just then, Jersey barked.

Okay, let's not just stand around. I see the leash. I see the door. Listen to me. I want OUT!

Will she bark all the time? I was still not convinced this was the dog for me.

Sandy knelt and clipped Jersey to a new leash. *That's an awfully small dog.* She looked even smaller standing on the floor near my feet.

"We'll wait here for you," Sandy said, looking up at me while she gently stroked Jersey's head.

I zipped up my raincoat and headed for the door carrying the bag of food and the crate. It was awkward, and I felt clumsy. Sandy said the crate would be easy to pop open and lock in place. With my back against the door, I tried pushing it open. *Wow, this door is heavy!* Then I realized the resistance was from the wind blowing against it from the other side. *The storm is getting worse.* After creating enough of an opening, I squeezed through, scraping my knuckles on the doorjamb. *Damn this thing.* I was already breathing heavily from the struggle and not enjoying one minute of this. Was it an omen?

I opened the back door of the car and wrestled with the metal contraption while the rain blew into the vehicle. I was getting frustrated, and my rubber raincoat certainly didn't breathe. I was soaked from sweat and rain. Sure was a lot of work, and I hadn't even gotten the dog yet. With a sigh of relief, I got the crate opened and positioned on the backseat. I put towels underneath to keep it from sliding around on the trip home and more inside the crate to make it comfortable.

Now back to the shelter for Cray-Kur. I couldn't help smiling as I remembered the moment I had come up with her name. I had wanted to honor my loving parents and the kindness of the Cray family, so I used part of my parents' last name and hyphenated it with the name Cray. It was different, and I liked it. And now, here I was, about to get my own dog with a most original name.

A sudden gust of wind interrupted my reverie as the rain pelted my face like particles of fine sand. *I hope this works out, especially after all this.* This moment felt like the time I was young, standing at the edge of a high-diving board for the first time, not knowing what it would be like until I did it. *Here goes nothing!*

Sandy was smiling as I returned to the front desk. Did she ever *not* smile? This time, I ignored the other dogs that wouldn't be going home with us. Us. I liked the sound of that.

Sandy laughed. "It's a mess out there, but Schipperkes don't mind the water. They are excellent swimmers!"

I forced a smile. I didn't really care right then, but it might be handy to know later.

"The puddles are pretty deep, and it's muddy, so I think I'll just carry her or else she'll be up to her belly in mud. Then I'll have one filthy dog inside one filthy car."

Cray-Kur was ready to go. She hadn't taken her eyes off me. I bent down, scooped her up, and cradled her in my arms. I thought about putting her inside my raincoat, but getting her out of it and into the crate without dropping her would be too tricky, especially in the wind and rain, so I decided just to hold her close to me. Cray-Kur had just been given her rabies shot, so I tried to hold her as gently as possible. I didn't want to hurt her.

Sandy walked with us to the door and gave me one last piece of advice. "She just got a heartworm shot, and she'll have to poop pretty soon. Here's her leash. Be careful out there!"

I leaned against the door and called, "Thanks. See you in a few days." I had to bring Cray-Kur back to the shelter in a couple of days regardless of whether I'd adopt her. She had to be spayed. It was part of the deal.

"Okay. Try to stay dry."

Once again, I forced the door open against the wind and looked down at this little black doggy in my arms. "Okay, Cray-Kur, you're going to get wet, but I'll do my best to protect you." I kissed her nose, and out we went.

This rain feels good, and I like being carried. Where are we going?

She smiled at me!

I walked as quickly as I could toward the car while trying to protect Cray-Kur. I looked down at her. She was looking up at me. She didn't flinch.

Was it even possible for the rain to be coming down harder than before? Sheets of wind-driven rain whipped across the muddy parking lot. I tried to cover Cray-Kur, but she got soaked; yet, she seemed oblivious to everything except me. The hood of my raincoat blew off my head. Strands of wet, gray hair blew across my face and stuck there while rainwater coursed down inside my raincoat.

"I'm sorry about this, little doggy. It'll be much nicer once we are home, where we'll be warm and dry, I promise."

I love this fresh air!

She kissed my face. Okay, maybe she was really licking the rain off me, but I let myself think it was kisses.

This water tastes different. Kind of salty. Not bad.

She looked very silly, almost like a different animal with her black hair all matted down to her small frame. She must have gotten soaked during Hurricane Katrina. Maybe she was used to this. It was the first of many times I wished she could talk.

I opened the car door and set her gently inside the crate. I wanted to dry her off but knew it would be impossible. We'd only get wetter.

"Okay, Cray-Kur, we are going for a ride in the car so I can get you home."

Cray-Kur seemed to know her new name. I smiled. I couldn't help it. This unique little black doggy with the original name intrigued me. Every time I talked to her, she looked at me. I was so eager to get her home, dry her off, and get acquainted.

A crate? You're joking. What's up with this? I never thought I'd have to be in another crate ever again. After the hurricane, it seemed that was how I went everywhere. But whatever. Let's just get out of here.

I waited a minute to see if the rain would let up to make driving easier or at least provide better visibility, but nothing changed. It was getting dark. I started the car, and off we went, back to my new home . . . and possibly hers.

I slowly pulled away from the building while keeping an eye on the crate as much as I could to be sure it didn't tip over. I knew this turf well, having run through this county land many times, but where the road had been and what was left of it was getting harder to see. I had to invent my own way to the main road. Funny, I'd often heard about roads washing out and had wondered where they went. Now I knew. They literally just washed away. My windshield wipers were in hyper mode and could barely keep up with the rain.

I angled the rearview mirror so I could see Cray-Kur. She hadn't made a sound. Not one bark. Nothing. She seemed to be taking this all in. We slowly bounced along as the car dipped into deep potholes that I thought were just puddles. *Please don't let it be like this tomorrow.*

What was normally a ten-minute drive between my home and the shelter became a thirty-minute adventure, but it gave Cray-Kur and me a chance to check each other out. Cray-Kur was sitting up, looking all around.

Are we there yet?

She was panting just a bit. Was she smiling, too? I explained where we were and where we were going. She listened.

"We're almost there, sweetie." I usually didn't use terms of endearment, but this was different. I immediately felt a great deal of responsibility for this little doggy.

Once my street came into view, I loosened the grip on the steering wheel. Up went the garage door, and I pulled inside, thankful to be out of that miserable wind and rain. Once my saturated raincoat and boots were peeled off, I opened the back door to lift my doggy out of the crate.

My doggy. I liked the sound of that. I finally had my own dog.

It was so easy to lift Cray-Kur. At the shelter, I hadn't noticed how light she was, and she hadn't resisted being picked up. I set her on the garage floor, and she shook her coat. I grabbed a towel and dried her thoroughly. She really enjoyed this pampering! *Gee, having a small dog that I could lift easily sure is convenient.*

"Welcome home, Cray-Kur!" She looked at me and cocked her head. Her ears pointed straight up.

I opened the door that led into the house from the garage and guided Cray-Kur to the bottom of a short flight of stairs. She shook her coat again and looked up at me.

What are these things? I've never seen a kennel like this.

"Haven't you ever seen stairs before?" She stood there. She didn't budge. Uh-oh. *Will this be a problem?* I carried her up a few steps and set her down on the landing. There were seven more steps to the main level.

Oh, I get it. It's a playground! Cool!

Cray-Kur paused a moment and then tentatively jumped up to the next step, then up to the next, and then she ran all the way to the top.

"Good girl!" My excitement was real. "Cray-Kur, come here. This is your bed!" I had bought a large, fleece doggy bed, and it looked so inviting that I plopped down on it, relieved to be home where it was warm and dry. I tried to coax her to join me. It was plush and cozy, but she wanted nothing to do with it. She was intrigued by yet another flight of stairs. This time, she ran all the way to the top and then back down.

I get called all these names. Sweetie. Jersey. Now Cray-Kur. What's up with that? But I like the way this woman holds me and talks to me. She's very gentle, so I guess I'm okay with all the names, including that odd one, Cray-Kur.

I stayed on the doggy bed studying her. She loved the stairs, and it certainly brought out the little athlete in her! I smiled.

Suddenly, I remembered what Sandy had said . . . that the medication would make Cray-Kur have to do her business. No sooner had I recalled her words than Cray-Kur ran into the living room and started sniffing around.

Too late.

I think you forgot Sandy told you I'd have to do some business. A dog can only hold it so long, even one as well-behaved as me.

She immediately squatted and pooped on my living room carpet! Two steps from that, she relieved herself by peeing on the hardwood floor.

Quickly, I scooped her up and ran outside into the rain without a raincoat or shoes. She pooped and peed *again!* Then I praised her and said, "Good job, Cray-Kur! This is where you'll do your business!"

I feel better now!

Once we were back inside, Cray-Kur ran up to the main level, and I followed her. She wagged her tail, happy that she had pleased me. What a tail! It was a sure gauge for her happiness. *Thump-thump-thump-thump* it went against a chair leg. From that day forward, Cray-Kur knew where to do her business when we went outside, and she always waited until she went to her spot.

A dog that was smart. Check.

Somebody who understands my needs. Check.

I peeled off my wet socks and headed for the white vinegar to clean up the mess and neutralize the odor. I didn't want a repeat performance. As I finished cleaning, I saw Cray-Kur watching me. "What is it, Cray-Kur?" She was staring at me.

I promise I won't do that again, but you have got to check in with me to see if I need to go out. I'll let you know if I do.

She was relieved of her need, and I smelled like salad dressing. She must have been laughing at all this silliness.

It was dinnertime, so I poured food into her bowl. Wow! Did she gobble that down! She didn't even look up. She kept her nose right in that dish. She must have gone a time without food during Hurricane Katrina. Again, I wished she could talk to me. I could only imagine.

Food, and lots of it! Yum! I know I'm being watched, but I can't get enough of this delicious food. And I don't have to share it with anyone!

We went through that first evening with me doing a lot of talking and Cray-Kur doing a lot of listening. I ended by telling her, "I'm your mom!"

She sure talks a lot.

She really liked my king-size bed, and I discovered she was quite the jumper when she leaped on it that first time. It was twice as high as she was tall.

It had been quite a day, and now it was time to turn in for the night. I had intended to bring her doggy bed up to the bedroom where she would sleep. But I was too late. She was already on my neatly made bed, pushing and pulling the covers with her paws as if making a nest. She fascinated me. Obviously, the sheets and blanket had to be just right for her.

My new house is pretty cool. It's a great big kennel with lots of stairs. Took me a minute to figure out what the heck I was supposed to do with them. In New Orleans, I didn't have stairs. But I figured these out. This place is one great big indoor playground just for me! Wow, thanks! I can run the way I was meant to run. I could do this all day! I think I'll call you Mom.

Mom was so easy to please! When I did things she liked, she rewarded me with sliced carrots. I showed her how smart I was. I showed her I could sit, lie down, stay, stand, and come . . . all on command. Of course, I was always rewarded, but the rewards weren't just treats. The smiles I brought to her face made it worth it. You see, the moment I met her, I could tell she was sad. I'd make her happy. I'd play by her rules and make her laugh. We'd all be happy.

I know Mom got me this doggy bed, but she has a huge bed that's much more comfortable. She can use the other bed since she likes it so much.

Once the sheets were exactly the way she wanted them, Cray-Kur curled up, and I climbed in next to her. I looked down at this gentle creature and softly stroked her fur. She let out a sigh and rolled on her back to let me rub her belly. We bonded. She must have been exhausted, and I was tired myself.

What a day! I am out of that other place and in a great home with my own king-size bed. I even liked that part Mom called ride-in-the-car, even though it's a very long word. I think I'll sleep just fine. Today is my lucky day.

It *had* been quite a day. Cray-Kur fell asleep almost immediately, and boy did that little doggy snore!

Lovable? Check.

I smiled. So far, so good. I didn't believe in luck, but I now understood what feeling lucky must be like. Maybe there was such a thing.

Chapter 2

Born to Run

Four in the morning came quickly. That was the time I normally got up to run. Call me regimented, but I always stayed on a schedule. People thought I was crazy to get up and run so early, but it was the very best part of the day. The town was so small that I could tell if I was late getting out to run, I would seethe same few cars every morning in the same places. Or if I had to wait for the train to finish going through town, I knew I was late. I waved to the usual early-morning folks: the garbage truck driver near the hospital, Cathy C. on her way to the gym, the one taxi driver in town, and the guy who rode his motorcycle almost all year, unless the roads had snow or ice on them. I waved to them all, and they waved back.

But now there was a new dimension to my life, and today was special. This was it. The big test. Time to see if Cray-Kur was really the runner Sandy had said she was. My doubts had already diminished, however, because of the way she ran up and down the stairs so effortlessly in our house.

I quickly got dressed and laced up my shoes. We went to the front door, where I had started keeping Cray-Kur's leash. She didn't seem to mind getting saddled up, as I called it. Thank goodness the forecasters were right. It had stopped raining.

I slipped a reflective vest over my head and clipped Cray-Kur's leash to her collar. Out the door we went, into the darkness of early morning in northern New England, where the air really is clean and crisp. I smiled and looked down to see how Cray-Kur was doing. She looked up at me and headed to her special place to relieve herself. Wow! Pretty smart! I was pleased and impressed. After I got her business picked up, it was time to run.

I cannot believe she is going to run with me. Not sure I understand why I must have this leash. Whatever. At least I get to run!

We ran slowly at first, as she needed to learn how to run with me holding her leash in my left hand. I wanted her to learn to stay on one side and not cross in front of me. I let her sniff all the new and unusual scents. When we got to the main street, I decided it was time to really open up. Wow! She was great! We ran about two miles at a pretty good clip toward a bridge over the river that ran through town. So far, so good.

Athletic? Check.

She can run. Check.

Uh-oh. Nope. Suddenly, Cray-Kur stopped in her tracks.

"What's wrong?"

A bridge. Moving water below. This isn't good. I remember what happened the last time I heard so much water moving past me. Just a few weeks ago. Katrina.

"Oh dear. I think I know what's going on with you," I said, looking down at Cray-Kur. "Up you go!" I scooped her up and carried her across the bridge.

"I wish you could talk. Maybe dogs can suffer from post-traumatic stress disorder," I wondered aloud. Surviving Hurricane Katrina was likely to leave scars. I wondered if there would be more.

I set her on the ground, and she was fine. "There you go. Let's run!" And off we went, as if nothing had happened.

Much better. Thanks, Mom. As soon as I sensed that moving water, I had a flashback, and it frightened me. I don't want to go anywhere near this water ever again.

We wrapped up a five-mile run, although it was obvious Cray-Kur could have gone a few more miles. That settled it.

We liked each other.

She was a great runner.

She was adorable, smart, and different.

She had spunk.

Done deal.

"So, how do you feel about being adopted?"

I have no idea what you said, but I really like the way you said it!

I like being with you, Mom. If I didn't know better, I'd say you're already crazy about me. Dogs know these things.

I really liked that run. I mean, I love running, but I haven't been able to run very far or very fast in a long time. It didn't really bother me that I had to run with you holding on to me. It was okay. Can you run as fast as me?

We didn't go near that moving water again for a while, which was fine with me. I couldn't wait to run again, and maybe we could go a lot farther and faster next time.

After eating breakfast together, I got dressed for work. My little art supply store was a one-woman shop, and I had considered bringing Cray-Kur with me. But I felt I needed to get to know her better and make sure she was well-behaved around people. It was just as important that she could handle being alone in the house. This was all so novel to me, and I was creating new routines as I went along.

I took Cray-Kur outside for a short business trip (that's what I called it, and she knew what I meant) before putting her in her crate in the living room. Until she got used to my work schedule, I thought I'd better keep her in her crate and then come home less and less frequently during the day to let her out. I was confident she would get used to the routine.

I couldn't wait for my work day to end, and I even put the *Closed* sign on the door earlier than usual. I headed home and pulled my trusty Volvo into the garage. I ran up the stairs two at a time. There she was. My doggy.

Cray-Kur stood up in her crate, her tail wagging vigorously.

Thump-thump-thump-thump it went against the side of the crate.

Boy, am I happy to see you! Let's go outside!

"Hi, Cray-Kur!" She seemed as happy to see me as I was to see her. Another great day with my new little doggy.

But there was something I still had to do. Cray-Kur needed to be spayed, so the next day when I got home from work, we walked around outside so she could take care of business. I wrestled the crate back into the car.

"We are going for a ride-in-the-car!"

Thump-thump-thump-thump.

Oh boy! A ride-in-the-car! But what's up with the crate again? Really? How long is this going to last? I really don't need this, but I'll do it for you. If I show you I can behave, will you put that thing away? I'll go along with it for a

while. Go ahead, Mom. Close the latch. You'll see I don't need this contraption.

I glanced in the mirror as I pulled out of the driveway, and Cray-Kur smiled at me. We headed toward the Humane Society, where I would leave her for two days. She seemed to enjoy riding in the car, but she was unaware of the destination.

We approached the shelter, and I was grateful the puddles had gotten smaller. Unfortunately, the parking lot was still a mess. I got out and opened the back door.

"Okay, I'm not going to put your leash on. It's too muddy to let you walk through this mess." And with that, I scooped her up in a motion that was becoming familiar to both of us.

Suddenly, Cray-Kur began to shake.

Wait a minute. I know this place, and I don't like it. Why are you bringing me back here? This is wrong. Mom? Hello? Talk to me. What's going on?

I tried to soothe her, but she continued to shake. We entered the building, and I set her down just inside the front door. Her shaking grew more violent.

Sandy was there to meet us. "How'd she do?"

"Wow, you were right," I said, beaming. "She's a runner! She's smart and happy, and I want to adopt her!" I glanced at Cray-Kur standing near me. Her trembling was intense. Now I was worried.

Sandy nodded knowingly. "That's great to hear. I had a good feeling about this one. Let's get her taken care of, and when she's ready for pickup in a few days, we'll have the adoption papers ready for you to sign."

"Wait, Sandy. She's scared to death. Look at her trembling. I can't leave her here." The truth was I didn't want to leave her at all. I needed to comfort her.

"I'll hold her in the back for a while and give her a sedative. She'll be fine. We see this a lot. Trust me, she'll be okay."

I had no choice. I had agreed to this condition as part of the adoption process. After all, she wasn't mine yet.

Sadness felt like a five-hundred-pound weight slowly crushing my heart. I handed the leash over to Sandy. I felt like I'd done the most horrible thing. Looking down at Cray-Kur was heartrending. She watched every move I made, listened to every word I said, and trembled from her nose to the tip of her waggy tail.

Mom???

I knelt down. "It's okay. I'll be back very soon. I promise," I whispered to Cray-Kur, my voice beginning to shake as much as her little body was shaking. I tried to calm myself and reassure her.

What's going on?

Cray-Kur stared at me.

Wasn't there another way to do this? She looked so scared. This was awful! It tugged at my conscience and my heart.

What are you doing? Where are you going? I don't understand.

I said goodbye and left. I felt like I was the meanest person on earth. I felt empty, sad, and suddenly very lonely. I missed her already! Now I wished it was raining to hide my tears.

All of a sudden, she was gone. Just like that. Where did she go? What's happening?

The house was strangely quiet and absent of her special energy. I couldn't wait to have her back, so I distracted myself by getting some special supplies for her. I went to an unfinished furniture store and bought a wooden stand with water and food bowls. From there, I went to the hardware store to get some varnish so it would look nice. Boy, I missed my dog! I couldn't stop thinking about her.

I loved being with Mom. She had learned how to treat me. I had her trained in no time! Everything was great.

Then we went for a ride-in-the-car, and now I'm in THIS PLACE. I feel sick. I know this place. I recognize the smells and sounds. It was where I was a day or two ago. What's going on?

Didn't Mom like me? Was she getting rid of me? I had been a good dog. I'm scared. I tried to beg her not to leave me here, but she couldn't understand. I love our house and running in the morning. I am so confused. I love our bed and all those stairs. I'll be good. Please come back!

What a betrayal! How could you do this to me? I really thought you liked me. Now they will euthanize me for sure if you won't keep me!

The two days of waiting until I could finally go back to the shelter were agonizing. I was totally focused on Cray-Kur and her needs. I'd gotten all the doggy supplies ever created— more toys, food, travel supplies, poop bags, and treats. I was so eager to officially adopt this little black doggy.

My friend Lynn, who occasionally helped me in my shop, drove me to the shelter so I could hold Cray-Kur in my arms for the ride home. I wanted to comfort and reassure her that we were going home together forever. Nothing would ever separate us.

Once inside the shelter, I introduced myself to another volunteer, and then I saw Sandy, smiling the smile of someone who had just brokered the deal of a lifetime.

"Hi, Sandy. Is she okay?"

Suddenly, from the back room, I could hear barking.

Back here, Mom, I'm back here! Come get me. Let's go for a ride-in-the-car. Let's get out of here!

"Ahhh . . . she recognizes your voice," Sandy said, grinning from ear to ear. "Let me go get her."

"There you are. I have missed you!" I dropped to my knees and kissed her nose. I was greeted with sweet doggy kisses.

Oh, Mommy, MOMMY! You're here! I've missed you. I love you. I'll kiss you more, but first . . . get me out of here!

I stood up. Cray-Kur was overjoyed. Her tail was wagging so fast I thought she would bruise Lynn's leg. *Thump-thump-thump-thump.* I hoped she didn't pee on Lynn or me in her excitement.

A few pen strokes that passed for a signature, a check to cover expenses and a donation, and I was ready. We both were. Off we went toward the car.

Wow. Mom never held me this close before! Easy there, Mom! Let's get out of here!

I passed Cray-Kur to Lynn, got in the passenger seat, and Lynn handed Cray-Kur back to me. The adoption was official, and it felt good. A woman and her wonderful new doggy heading to their home. Life was good. Cray-Kur licked my face all the way back. There was no rainwater this time, just sweet doggy kisses. I held her closely, being careful about her tender belly, and I kissed the top of her head.

"I love you, Cray-Kur," I whispered. I felt so much affection for this creature. Her ears pointed straight up. "I love your little bat ears!" I was ecstatic. It was then that Cray-Kur earned the nickname Little Miss Bat Ears. She didn't seem to mind.

I kissed her, and she kissed me back. She called me Little Miss Bat Ears. Who cares? She could've called me Godzilla because all that mattered was that she was back, and I was leaving that place.

I am SO happy to see her. Now we are going for a ride-in-the-car. When I get home, I can run up and down the stairs, get up early and run outside, and sleep in my own big bed. Life is wonderful again.

Chapter 3

My Tummy Hurts

Cray-Kur quickly learned the routines. We would get up early in the morning and run. I swore she could tell time, because at 3:45 a.m., she would leap off the bed and let me know it was time to go. She got used to running over that bridge in a matter of weeks. Then, after breakfast, I'd get ready for work. Cray-Kur stayed in her crate those first few weeks, and then I tried leaving her loose in the house. She got used to being alone all day, and she was fine. Success! No accidents!

Well, it's about time! I am smart, and I'd never do my business in this place. It's my home! I'm so happy!

Thump-thump-thump-thump.

Hurricane Katrina had devastated New Orleans. It hadn't been that long ago—just a matter of weeks had passed since one of the worst natural disasters in US history. The nightly news continued to show homes destroyed by the flooding. Whenever coverage of the event was on TV, I stopped what I was doing to watch and see if I could spot Cray-Kur. I knew the odds were high that I would see her, but I couldn't help it. I had to watch. I wondered what the circumstances were like for her in the South, who her family was, and why she had been abandoned. I wanted to know more. Boy, I wished she could talk!

I had fallen in love with Cray-Kur, or Crazy Cray-Kur, as I sometimes called her when she did goofy, silly, crazy things to entertain me. And what a goofball she was! She made me laugh out loud.

Sometimes, I would get down on all fours and pretend to charge her. She'd play along. She was fun and crazy to the bone, so I started calling her Crazy Bones. She made me feel young again. I think she was as crazy about me as I was about her.

Crazy Bones. There she goes again. I've got another name. I don't get it, but she says it with so much love that it's okay. She can call me anything.

Crazy Bones proved to be a very fast learner. I taught her more commands: Roll over! Lie down! Fetch! I rewarded her with small treats . . . and of course, she would do anything for a treat!

Wow, I would do anything for Mom. She plays with me, and I taught her to reward me with treats after I did what she wanted. She's pretty smart that way.

I reinforced the stay command every time I fed her. I would put her food out and tell her, "Stay!" She would stay until I released her by saying, "Go get your food," which was accompanied with a wave of my hand and a nod of my head in the direction of the food. Over time, I released her with only the nod of my head. She was quite impressive. She would stay motionless until I released her, watching my every move, even drooling in anticipation of her release.

One time, though, I put the food down, told her to stay, and then went upstairs to change my clothes. Five minutes later, I came down and found her still waiting . . . and there was the world's longest string of drool connecting her mouth to the floor. I was horrified that I had forgotten to release her, but what a good doggy she was for waiting to be released. I never did *that* again!

I took my mom running every morning, and she took me along almost everywhere she went. She had a small but lovely group of friends who liked me. I loved the music in her house. It reminded me of another place and time.

Part of our day was eating together, especially after our early-morning runs. Whenever Mom finished eating yogurt from a big container, she would set it on the floor and let me lick it. What a treat! It was about the only food she shared with me. As much as I loved her, I am not sure I would have shared my food with her or anybody, for that matter. As a Hurricane Katrina refugee, I learned a thing or two about survival.

Anyway, back to the yogurt. I would carry the container in my teeth to a more comfortable dining area like the family room, which was carpeted. Steadying the container between my

front paws, I'd lick it clean as far as my head would go into the container. My tongue could reach most of it. It was great entertainment for Mom. One time, I picked up the container in my teeth and lifted it. It slipped and slid completely over my head. I'm not sure why that was so funny. All I was trying to do was get that very last taste of yogurt, but Mom thought it was hysterical.

During the day, I'd leave the stereo on to help cover any noises from outside that might upset Cray-Kur or make her bark. I listened to contemporary jazz on the radio. She really seemed to enjoy the music of Joe Sample and Diana Krall.

In the afternoon when I got home from work, we'd take a walk so Cray-Kur could do her business. Then we'd visit our nice neighbor, Uncle Roland, an older gentleman whose wife had passed soon after I'd bought my home. We'd pass his house on our business trips, and in warmer weather, we'd stop for a while and sit with him on one of his lawn chairs just inside his overhead garage door. We'd talk about the day and watch the clouds drift by as the sun lowered itself onto the horizon.

I really like Uncle Roland. Such a gentle man and he has a dog named Kisses. Mom and I did nice things for him. When the weather turned cold, we would return from our early-morning run and get Uncle Roland's newspaper from the end of his driveway and tuck it inside his front door so he didn't have to leave the warmth of his house. He appreciated that. I could tell he loved me so I would give him plenty of love and kisses.

After dinner, we'd watch TV in bed. I always talked to Cray-Kur and told her what was going on. It didn't matter what I said. She would listen, watch me, and cock her head from one side to the other. She had such expressive ears, and Little Miss Bat Ears always knew when I spoke directly to her. There was no doubt that she understood me. We had become one. I relied on her for companionship, and we needed each other.

I really like being with Mom. I always understand her. She needs me.

In my family, we all had nicknames, and Crazy Cray-Kur had morphed into Crazy Bones. Crazy Bones sometimes got shortened to just Bones, which sometimes became Bonus. Or Bonesey. I used all her nicknames interchangeably. A study of etymology or linguistics was not needed. It was simply the evolution of a nickname. At any rate, and with any name, she knew I was talking to her because Crazy Bones was a very smart doggy! "Right, Crazy Bones?"

I'm not sure where the crazy part of Crazy Bones came from, and I'm even less sure where the bones part came from. It didn't really matter. She entertained me, I entertained her endlessly, and we took really good care of each other.

I was curious about Schipperkes. I'd never heard of this breed, and people often questioned me about it. Research on the American Kennel Club website taught me Schipperkes (pronounced *skipper-kees*) were bred to chase rodents on barges in northern Europe. Their jet-black coat, stealthy movements, and strong but small bodies made them perfect work dogs. I could easily imagine Cray-Kur chasing anything that moved, but I couldn't picture her harming another living creature. I suppose it was all about the hunt as well as her protective instincts.

Life had a renewed spirit with this fresh new dimension in my routine. I was happier than I'd been in a very long time. It became less important to keep a rigid schedule because I enjoyed being with Cray-Kur so much. I had fun introducing her to my friends, and she developed a wonderful extended family. In addition to Lynn, there were Auntie Kim and Uncle Jimmy, who had two big Labs of their own. They took an instant liking to Cray-Kur. Auntie Kelly had not liked dogs until she met Cray-Kur. And there were others: Uncle Freddy, Auntie Tina, and the two families with whom she stayed when I had to travel. The first family was Kimberly, Rick, and their teenage boys. The second was Dee and Kevin. These friends had dogs, and I trusted them with Cray-Kur.

A few times, I got to stay with Kimberly and her family. I loved staying there and playing with their big dogs! Nobody ever told me I wasn't a big dog, so I'd play tug-of-war with a rope toy and one of the dogs. Everybody thought this was funny. Kimberly and Rick let me sleep with them in their bed. I insisted on it. Rick tried to get me to sleep on a dog bed, but it didn't work.

Mom had spoiled me. I always got my way at their house. They had a really big home with even more stairs than we had. They were cool.

Cray-Kur playing with Kimberly's dogs.
Photo courtesy Kimberly Faustino.

Dee and Kevin were cool, too. They loved animals, and they had no problem whatsoever with my sleeping in their bed, as long as my collar and all its tags were removed. Kevin said the jingling kept him awake at night. Well, I have to tell you something. Somebody kept me awake snoring. Not naming names here, but . . .

On occasion, we took short vacations. Sometimes we would stay with friends and family, and at other times, we would stay in a dog-friendly hotel.

People seemed to like me. If they didn't? So what. I felt more and more calm as I got older. Mom said I had mellowed. I was content. I think Mom had mellowed, too, and I knew she was content.

Mom loved to watch me run, no matter where we were. She would laugh and sometimes roll around on the floor with me. Other times, I had fun letting her chase me. When I would drop and roll onto my back, she'd ask me, "Do you want a rubbie?" She would rub my belly and give me kisses. I trusted her.

That first Christmas, holiday cards were addressed to both of us! I did something I swore I would never do: I bought something Christmassy for Cray-Kur to wear. It was a red-and-white fluffy elastic collar that had three or four bells on it. It fit perfectly around her neck, and it stood out beautifully against her black coat.

I can't believe Mom bought that thing. I couldn't stand it. Every time I moved, the bells jingled. That collar didn't last long. I began to remove all but one bell. Please don't ever do that again!

Every now and then, someone would look quizzically at Cray-Kur and ask what breed she was.

"She's a Schipperke, but she has a little terrier in her, which gives her a longer, straighter tail." I could now speak a bit more knowledgeably about my dog. I'd add that I rescued her after Hurricane Katrina and hoped people would understand that she had gone through a lot of trauma in her young life. I also explained that she was suspicious of strangers and they shouldn't get too close to her.

You rescued me?

One day when I came home from work, Cray-Kur wasn't at the door where she usually greeted me.

"Crazy Bones, I'm home!" Normally, she could hear the garage door open so she knew I was home, and that was her cue to run downstairs to meet me. But on this day, she wasn't there. I quietly walked up the stairs.

Still no sign of Cray-Kur, but I did hear voices. Who was that?

Well, there was Cray-Kur, stretched out on the bed. She had found the remote control to the TV and played with it or stepped on it but somehow had turned it on. With the TV on, she hadn't heard me. Or maybe she was too busy watching *Oprah* and getting some good relationship advice.

"Crazy Bones, you goofball! You had me worried when you didn't meet me at the door!"

There you are! I want a rubbie, Mom!

When Cray-Kur rolled on her back to get her belly rubbed, her tail wagged just as vigorously as when she was standing, but instead of the characteristic *thump-thump-thump-thump*, it went *swish-swish-swish-swish* on the bed.

On the weekends, we'd go for very long walks early in the morning instead of running. Occasionally, I had friends over in the afternoon. Cray-Kur was wary, not trusting new people at all. She was protective and usually put herself squarely between me and whoever visited, barking to express her discontent.

Um, excuse me. This is my mom, and I don't like that you are standing so close. Back off! I was very assertive.

Cray-Kur would snarl sometimes, but as she got to know my friends and saw how nice they were toward me, she was okay. I explained her behavior to lots of people, saying, "She's just doing her job to protect me." I called her my Protector Doggy.

My closest friends didn't undergo the scrutiny that more casual visitors did. I would simply tell Cray-Kur in advance who was coming.

"Guess who is coming over! Auntie Kim is coming over!"

Thump-thump-thump-thump.

Then Cray-Kur would run to the door in anticipation.

"Sorry, Crazy Bones, she's coming over later, like in about four hours." I learned not to announce guests until just before their arrival. When I had parties, she showed off her social skills. She knew who loved dogs.

I love it when Mom has friends visit our house. I get lots of attention!

Cray-Kur turned out to be a great judge of character. I'd watch her around strangers and follow her lead. If the hair on her back stood up or if she snarled—even if *I* had no reason to be concerned—I would cut short my conversation and move on. My unexpected lesson on her ability to judge people came one day when I took Cray-Kur on a walk through the annual arts festival in our town. The main road was closed, and it was fun to look at all the exhibits. Now and then a young child would point to Cray-Kur and say, "Doggy," and I was pleased when Cray-Kur allowed herself to be approached by innocent children. However, a harmless-looking stranger approached and muttered something about a "rat dog." I took offense to it, and Cray-Kur *really* didn't like him or his comment. She snarled, and I quickly crossed the street to avoid a confrontation. From that point on, I went by her instincts, not mine.

"You're a good Protector Doggy," I'd tell her.

Crazy Bones was very inquisitive and loved to explore, and I mean beyond the usual sniffing around under shrubs and inside people's shoes.

I didn't realize just how inquisitive she was until one afternoon when I came home from work and she didn't run to greet me. Instead, she was curled up on the couch.

Oh my gosh. My stomach is killing me. Please don't rub my belly. I feel sick.

This was so uncharacteristic and clearly not good. I could see she was lethargic and didn't want her belly rubbed. *That* was what made me worried. What had happened?

"Bones, how about just a little taste of food?" I tried to hand-feed her.

Nope, can't handle it.

She tried to vomit, and that's when I noticed something hanging from her mouth. I tried to pull what looked like a strand of yarn, but it wouldn't come out. Whatever it was, it was wrapped around her insides.

That hurts.

"What happened? Bones, I will take care of you." I was in a panic. I called the vet, then carefully carried Crazy Bones to the car, where I set her carefully on the front seat. She didn't move. *Oh, dear God. Please protect her. Don't let anything bad happen to her.*

I sped across town to the animal hospital. Immediately, the vet took a CAT scan and a series of X-rays. It seemed Cray-Kur had found a loose Berber carpet thread and started eating it. As she ate, it kept unraveling, and she kept eating. About eight feet of Berber carpet thread was surgically removed.

Cray-Kur required four days of hospitalization, and I visited her several times each day, checking in before work, during my lunch hour, at dinnertime, then just before bedtime. She'd hear my voice and try to sit up, but she couldn't at first.

Mom, I'm not sure what happened! I saw this piece of skinny rope that reminded me of rope toys, so I started eating it. The texture felt good on my tongue. I kind of remember getting sick.

I have a wonderful vet taking care of me. Her name is . . . get this . . . Dr. CAT! At first, I was worried she hadn't noticed I'm a dog. But then I learned those were her initials. She kisses my nose, and I kiss her back because I like her. Dr. CAT is a great vet, but I want to go back to my house.

Cray-Kur's belly was shaved and sutured in a five-inch line. She was kept on an IV of water, food, and antibiotics.

"Cray-Kur's very lucky," Dr. Christina Adriana Terry explained. "We're glad you caught it when you did. She's getting more responsive, and I think she'll be okay, but she needs to be kept quiet until her incision is healed enough to go home. By the way, she is very muscular. She must get a lot of exercise."

I smiled, and for the first time in many days, I felt everything would be okay. Dr. Terry's reassurance let me get some sleep in that big empty bed of ours. I missed her.

Before Cray-Kur was discharged, I replaced all the carpets in *our* house and made sure there were no loose ends of carpet thread anywhere.

Thank goodness we had dodged that bullet! It was a scary time for both of us.

Chapter 4

Snow!

In northern New England, we had huge snowfalls that began as early as October and lasted into April or May. I'll always remember the first time Cray-Kur experienced snow. We were going out for an early-morning weekend walk.

When Mom opened the front door to head out for our morning routine, there were six or seven inches of this white stuff! It was up to my belly, but it was easy to walk through . . . magical and powdery, as I found when I cautiously stepped in it the first time. It stuck to my paw. I had to shake the snow off that paw, but then it stuck to the other front paw, so I had to shake

it off that one. Every step required shaking. But I got used to the snow pretty fast and stopped trying to shake it off.

I sniffed and sniffed at the snow. I sniffed it all the way to the end of the driveway. I tasted it and discovered it was like water! I licked my way down our little white road. Yum!

I was so glad the plow guy hadn't come yet. Fresh snow was so beautiful. So pristine. It was part of the natural beauty of where I lived.

Sometimes the snow was too deep for running on the sidewalks. On those days, I'd put on my snowshoes, and we would head out the back door toward the woods and follow the miles and miles of snowmobile trails.

One morning, we opened the door to discover a huge snowfall had dumped two feet of new snow on top of the snow already there from the previous storm. It was just before the sun came up. I loved this time of day. As the sun rose, the color of the sky changed by the minute.

Cray-Kur got so excited that she'd run in circles and carve paths in the snow.

Come on, Mom. Hurry up!

She never put me on a leash when we went snowshoeing, and I never went far away from her.

It was always so quiet among the tall evergreen trees. Sometimes when the snow was really deep, I'd follow Mom and leap from each imprint of her snowshoe to the next, then to the next. Other times, I ran ahead. She always laughed when we went snowshoeing. When I took big leaps, she said I reminded her of the gazelles she saw in Africa leaping their way across the Serengeti, whatever that is. But I loved it, and Mom would sing made-up songs about me.

It brought me great joy to watch Crazy Bones run ahead of me in the woods. The snow wouldn't be as deep there because it got caught on all the branches high above us.

I loved to scamper ahead of Mom. One time I ran ahead of her, but I didn't see that a large clump of fluffy white snow had broken loose from a high bough. It drifted silently down and landed with a soft splat on my head. I was startled and completely covered in snow. The still morning air was broken by Mom's laughter.

"Crazy Bones!" Mom yelled, laughing loudly. "You are totally white. I wish I had a camera!"

I laughed at her laughing at me. If you don't think dogs laugh, think again. Mom was crazy. Absolutely crazy about ME!

I shook off all the snow and continued sniffing and exploring on that beautiful, absolutely glorious morning. Just Mom and me. Life was good!

There was a small lake near our house. When it was safe, Mom and I would walk across the ice toward the farm on the other side. It was so much fun! Snowmobilers sometimes drove on the frozen lake. We could hear them from far away because they were so loud and the air was so quiet. As soon as they saw Mom's orange safety vest (and I wore one, too), the snowmobilers slowed down, waved, and kept a safe distance. I wanted to chase them, but Mom told me to stay with her. I don't think the snowmobiles could have gone as fast as me.

Later, back at the house, we would sit on the floor near the wood-burning stove, and I would snuggle up beside my mom. The heat would dry the melted snow from my fur. It felt so good.

Mom and I were inseparable. Sometimes, Mom read the Sunday paper or did puzzles while I'd fall asleep next to her. It was the epitome of contentment. Mom felt the same way.

Thump-thump-thump-thump.

In the winter, I usually spent Sunday afternoons relaxing with the Sunday edition of the *Portland Herald Press* and the *Maine Sunday Telegram*. I enjoyed tackling the crossword puzzles and Sudoku logic games. Following our long walks in the snowy woods, I knew Cray-Kur would be tired and wouldn't have to go outside again for a long time, so I'd indulge in the coziness of our home. I'd bundle up in flannel pajamas, put on my wool socks, and create a pillow "fortress" on the floor in front of the woodstove. While it was a bit of a challenge to read the paper or work the puzzles with Cray-Kur occasionally rearranging the papers with her paws as she stretched and turned, I managed. Or I simply gave up and fell asleep myself. I was so glad I rescued her.

I'm so glad I rescued her.

Chapter 5

The Beach

I thought I knew everything there was to know about my dog, but there were always more surprises, the biggest of which came when I started taking her to Long Sands Beach in York, Maine that first summer together. There was nothing as glorious as watching the sunrise while running on the beach. I think Crazy Bones felt the same way.

Look at all the water! I think I've seen this somewhere before. The water looks as blue as the sky, and it even smells and tastes familiar, although it is a bit too salty to drink. The breeze is nice, too. I like it here. The sand feels so soft under my paws. And look at all those

birds on the beach! Thanks, Mom. This place is awesome!

I would run up the beach and back—a five-mile run. But for Cray-Kur, it was a longer run because she would run ahead, then run back to me, then run ahead, then back to me. She ran four times the miles I ran. I don't remember ever laughing while running, but this was different. I was so happy watching Cray-Kur run on the beach. When she ran at top speed, her ears would be angled straight back, making her as aerodynamic as possible.

"Let's go in the water, Crazy Bones!" I waded into waist-deep water holding her in my arms.

"Okay, let's see what you can do!"

Are you kidding? I am a natural-born swimmer, and if you let me go, you'll see!

"Okay, here you go. I'll be right here if you need me. I won't let anything happen to you." Boy, did I love this dog. She was so much fun!

Carefully, tentatively, I let go of her. "Go, Crazy! Swim!"

I haven't done this in . . . forever! This is great fun. Not sure why Mom calls this dog-

paddling, though. It's fun to catch the waves just before they break.

Crazy Bones was an amazing swimmer, and I was the one trying to keep up! Then I remembered what Sandy had told me when I adopted this little athlete. Schipperkes were good swimmers. Indeed, she was.

"Let's ride the waves," I said, assuming she knew what I meant.

Come ride the waves with me!

This water is different. I haven't seen waves like this before. I know I've been in some big lake somewhere, but this was different. This is more fun. Come on, Mom!

We'd bodysurf back to the shore, head back out, and do it over and over and over again. I wondered if she'd ever been in Lake Pontchartrain, the very large lake in New Orleans. Or maybe she had to swim through the flooded streets of New Orleans.

There usually weren't many people on the beach at sunrise, especially in early spring when the water temperature was in the high 50s, but the few beachcombers out there had stopped to watch this middle-aged woman romping in the surf with her dog. I'm sure it provided plenty of amusement for them while we got lots of exercise.

"You are such a great swimmer," I said, catching my breath as we climbed out of the surf. Cray-Kur shook the salty water off her body.

That was awesome. Thanks, Mom. Hey, look!

Cray-Kur saw a dozen shorebirds about a hundred feet down the beach and decided to chase them. I let her run. Ears pinned straight back, she charged down the beach. The birds immediately took off as soon as they saw her coming. She just wanted to chase them, not attack them. It was simply the joy of running and playing the game of chase.

When we were both tired from running and swimming, I'd tell Cray-Kur we were going for a ride-in-the-car. Her ears would perk up, and she'd walk up the beach beside me toward the sand dunes to the outdoor shower. I'd lift her little body under the spray of water, always grateful that Cray-Kur was so easy to wash. Once the salt water was rinsed from her fur, I'd wrap her in a towel and carry her to the car for the short drive home.

That felt good, Mom!

Chapter 6

Hanging Out with Grandpa

On the one-year anniversary of Hurricane Katrina, the images of New Orleans reappeared on the nightly news showing the rebuilding of a broken, ravaged city. Again, and again, I watched every frame of footage hoping I'd see her. I had become very curious about Cray-Kur's past. Maybe this was how adopting parents felt when they wanted information about a child's medical history.

Mom seemed to watch TV a lot. The images looked vaguely familiar to me, but I didn't have that much interest in watching TV. She seemed to be looking for something.

I began the quest for information back at the Humane Society. I learned that any healthy pet that had not been claimed within the first two weeks following the hurricane was sent to one of many animal shelters that were accepting refugees from Katrina. There was even an active phone number for people still trying to locate their pets.

Mom told me she learned the name of the organization that had arranged my flight from Tennessee to New Hampshire. She had a number of heartbreaking conversations with volunteers in shelters in Tennessee as she searched for my owner. She had lots of questions, like what was the name of my family? Of course, she always asked about Jersey. She sent photos of me to these wonderful volunteers in case anyone ever went to them in search of their lost dog. She included her name, address, and telephone number.

So, I had to wonder. Why was she doing this? Was she trying to get rid of me? That didn't make sense, but she seemed intent on this project. It was confusing.

What if she found my original family and they wanted me back? I vaguely remember

them. I recall they were nice. If she found them, what would she do? What would happen to me? We had bonded.

I had a great house with lots of stairs, great food, and I loved this crazy person I'd rescued. I knew this was really bothering Mom, so I gave her lots of kisses. I'd been through a lot, and somehow I just knew everything would be fine. I loved her unconditionally.

I had been feeling a bit guilty and confused, but as time passed and I hadn't heard anything, I felt I was somehow off the hook. After all, if I had learned something about her roots, wouldn't I feel compelled to do something? Deep down, I was afraid I would end up giving Cray-Kur back to her owner. But as the saying goes, no news is good news, so I began to relax. Life resumed its normal cadence, and we continued our adventures together, like taking trips in the car.

Sometimes Mom and I would drive to New Jersey, where she grew up, to see her parents and other family members. There sure were a lot of them. Mom believed family was whoever she chose it to be, not something based on biology. She called her parents my grandparents, and

they liked that. Mom and I visited Grandma and Grandpa, Uncle Lee, Aunt Maureen, Cousin Karl, Cousin Carol (who always knew just how to scratch my chin!), Uncle Jim, and Cousin Billy. I met my cousin, Chester, Aunt Anne's basset hound. He was my only canine cousin.

Grandpa was already in his eighties when I first met him and Grandma. They had visited our home in New Hampshire. I loved to hang out with them. I was their first granddog. Grandpa had always loved dogs, but I was special.

Another reason it was fun to go to New Jersey was because there were acres and acres of land where I could run and play. Grandma and Grandpa's house was in Bedminster, and I could run all around the family farm, where there was so much land and unusual buildings called barns with so many interesting new smells. Sometimes we would go to Bernardsville, where Mom went to high school. We would walk through that little town and explore areas where many of her classmates used to live. She enjoyed the nostalgia, and I enjoyed the walks. Mom told me stories about the places we went. I could tell this place was special to her.

There were always plenty of people to play

with in New Jersey. My favorite was Grandpa. I wasn't sure who enjoyed playtime more, Grandpa or me. He and Grandma always let me sit on their laps. Sometimes Grandpa would sneak a little food to me under the table at dinnertime, even though he denied doing this.

Mom would say, "Dad, stop that! I don't want her to be a table beggar!"

Grandpa would look at me and wink. We understood each other. We had a special connection that made it okay.

Thump-thump-thump-thump.

I loved our visits to New Jersey, but eventually, we had to head back to New Hampshire.

Chapter 7

A Connection to My Past

Big moments in life rarely come with announcements. The sudden death of a loved one. Holding the winning lottery ticket. Getting rear-ended at a red light. Twins!

A big moment in my life arrived without fanfare on an otherwise normal Saturday afternoon. In the mail, there was a handwritten envelope with a return address I didn't recognize. Whom could this be from? I opened it and stood there reading the most amazing letter:

Dear Miss Elizabeth,

My name is Charles. I lived in New Orleans until the big hurricane washed my life away. I had a small black dog named Jersey. I tried to find her after the flood. I looked in every shelter and hoped she was taken to a safer place. I think you have my dog.

My kids and I adored Jersey, and we miss her. But we are living in Tennessee now because our home couldn't be salvaged. I hope you get my letter and that you write back.

Jersey is a wonderful dog. God bless you,

Charles de LaSepps and family

I stood there stunned. I felt an amazing connection to . . . what? To this guy Charles? I felt I'd come into a treasure trove of doggy genealogy. I wanted to tell Cray-Kur. What a silly thought! Wait. I could let her smell the letter! But then what? She couldn't tell me what I wanted to know. Questions cascaded through my mind. What do I do now? Who should I tell? Should I just keep it to myself?

Hmmm. I guess I should respond to Charles. Didn't I want to know all about Cray-Kur? Didn't I watch endless hours of news footage covering Hurricane Katrina hoping to see my dog? I really should write back.

I felt so conflicted. What a can of worms I had opened! What if Charles wanted her back? I couldn't part with my doggy. But he didn't say he wanted her back. Darn it! I wish I had never written that first letter. What had I done?

I went back and forth for several days trying to figure out what to do. Should I write to him? After all, he had written to me. I wanted to ask him questions about Cray-

Kur's past life. I could enclose photos and tell him about her new life. Still, I was nervous. It didn't sound like he wanted his lost dog back, but I had second thoughts that kept me awake at night . . . millions of what-ifs. But I'd started this communication, so I began to write:

Dear Charles,

It was wonderful hearing from you. I believe I have your dog. As I understand it, she was sent to a series of shelters before being flown to the seacoast region of New Hampshire for a new life.

She had a tag that said JERSEY, but I renamed her Cray-Kur, which comes from a combination of the first syllable of my parents' last name and the last name of a family that was very kind to me when I needed kindness.

Cray-Kur is a loving companion. I'm sure she learned to be a good listener and a great friend from being with you. She runs with me every morning, and sometimes, I'll take her into the woods or to the beach. I am sending you recent photos of her.

Please tell me about her past—were you the original owner or was Cray-Kur somewhere else first? I have so many questions.

Thanks for writing, Charles. I look forward to hearing from you.

Elizabeth

Without a pause that could stop my momentum, I crossed the street to the mailbox and pulled open the mail drop. I stood there holding it open, knowing that once I dropped the letter in, that was it. What would happen next? Would I regret it?

"One, two, three." And I dropped the letter in the box.

Now I had to wait. Would I ever hear from Charles again? He sounded nice, but what did I really know about him? Wouldn't his kids want their dog back? I immediately regretted my action. I could never give up this little dog, but what if the roles were reversed? Good Lord, what had I done?

Time passed without hearing anything from Charles. I was disappointed and relieved. Life went back to normal, but I lived with the nagging fear that someday I'd hear from Charles or . . . maybe he'd just show up and want his dog. He had my address. I should've used my work address. I hadn't thought this thing through, and now the possibility of giving up Cray-Kur was weighing on me. Was I overthinking this?

Weeks passed. The season changed. I busied myself with routines. Cray-Kur and I got up early and ran, then I'd go to work. I'd come home. We'd go for a walk, eat, relax, then we'd go to bed. We had a nice, simple life. But I couldn't let go of the *what if*. . . that was hanging over me every day. What if Charles wanted his dog back?

Then one night after dinner, it all caught up with me, and I started to cry. I sat on the couch and Cray-Kur jumped up to be near me. I looked at her. "What have I done? I love you so much and don't want to lose you." I held her closely. She had become the focus of my life. She kissed me.

"You are so special. I love you, Crazy."

It's okay, Mom. Whatever is bothering you, it's okay. I'll be right here by your side.

More time passed and I thought less and less about my communication with Charles. Nothing came in the mail. I guessed that was the end of it.

Chapter 8

Happy New Beginnings and Sad Endings

It happened quickly. Too quickly for some of my skeptical friends, but not for me. I was ready. Through a mutual friend, I met a man from Virginia named Ernie.

Mom told me about Ernie. I wasn't sure who or what that was, but then I met him, and that was important. You see, I'm a much better judge of character than Mom is. It's one of my many gifts.

I could tell Ernie liked dogs, and I knew he even had one because my keen sense of smell detected another canine on Ernie's clothes.

When Ernie talked to me, I could hear a smile in his voice. He treated me like the intelligent

being that I am. I liked Ernie a lot. He would fly to New Hampshire in one of those big metal birds I'd see in the sky. He came to visit me a lot because he liked me. I guess he liked Mom, too.

Mom liked Ernie so much that she referred to him as Daddy when she spoke to me. There she goes again! He had a name. Why didn't she use that one? I really didn't understand the need for all these names, but I guess that's just the way Mom is, so I went along with the name Daddy. *Whatever!*

Whenever Ernie would fly up for a visit, the anticipation was great for both Cray-Kur and me. Shortly before he'd arrive in his rental car, I'd tell Cray-Kur that Daddy was coming. We'd stand by the kitchen door and watch for him.

Daddy arrived in a different car every time he visited us. Mom and I watched and waited until we saw him driving down our dirt road. As soon as the car came to a stop in the driveway, Mom would open the door, and I would burst outside and run as fast as I could to the car. As soon as Daddy saw me, he'd open his car door so I could jump in his lap.

"Crazy Bones!" he'd exclaim. He even laughed when he said it. "Hi, Crazy!"

I was so excited! I didn't care what he called me! I would give him as many kisses as he'd allow; then I would jump out and run around and around in circles in the driveway. Daddy called it doing doughnuts.

I loved it when Daddy came to visit. He was always smiling, and he loved to sneak me treats when Mom wasn't looking. I could tell he was always happy to see me. He would laugh and say, "Crazy Bones!" over and over again.

Soon Daddy became a fixture in our lives. One time, Mom and I went for a ride-in-the-car from New Hampshire to New Jersey, and Daddy drove there from Virginia. New Jersey was somewhere in the middle. Daddy brought his dog, a miniature schnauzer named Scooty. We were the same age and the same size. Scooty was a bit more timid, so if she didn't grab a treat that was thrown to her, ha! I'd get it. Never let a morsel of food get away! I'd learned that a long time ago back in . . . Where was that?

Scooty turned out to be a great sister. Sometimes I'd chase her through the house. Then we'd entertain anyone who was watching and reverse direction. I taught her new ways to get attention.

Okay, now all you do is go up to somebody you trust, look sweetly at them, sit for a moment, then roll over on your back. They will realize you want your belly rubbed. It's simple. They fall for it every time. Watch!

And with that, I showed her how it was done.

I walked over to Daddy, sat on the floor in front of him, then slowly, I rolled over on my back, watching him the whole time.

"Ohhhhhh! I know what YOU want!" Daddy would say. "You want a rubbie!" And with that, he would reach down and rub my belly. My tail wouldn't stop wagging, even while I was on my back.

Swish-swish-swish-swish.

Go ahead, Scooty. You try it, I said, getting up and walking away.

Scooty looked at me. I could read her mind: *Seems simple enough, but I've never done this before.*

Go ahead and try it, I said again. *You'll see. I've got them trained pretty well.*

Sure enough, Scooty chose a spot on the living room carpet in front of Daddy. It looked like a good place to have her belly rubbed. She sat down, rolled over, and voilà!

"Oh, my goodness," Daddy, said. "Look who wants *her* belly rubbed!" And so it began. I had trained Scooty, and she had trained Daddy. Everybody thought it was funny. I knew it was just smart. There was much more to teach Scooty.

Ernie and I were both pleased that our doggies got along well. They had an instant affection for each other, and it made our visits to New Jersey so much more enjoyable. They would chase each other and get tired. That, in turn, guaranteed they would sleep well through the night.

Visiting my parents was always special, but as they aged and their health issues increased, I knew their years were numbered. I increased the frequency of my visits. Ernie drove up with Scooty as often as possible, and it was nice to have him there for moral support. I also wanted to make sure my father got to know Ernie because they were the two most important men in my life. Crazy Bones and Scooty always served as delightful distractions for everyone.

During one visit to New Jersey, I could see Grandpa had become very frail. It was a

dramatic change from the last time I'd seen him. Mom brought him home from the hospital so he could spend his final days in the place he had built—the place he loved most—his home. I went on that trip to the hospital because I had a special job. I comforted him and made him happy on that ride-in-the-car home. Grandpa sat in the backseat with me, and Grandma sat up front with Mom. We stayed in New Jersey several weeks for that final visit with Grandpa.

In his last weeks, Grandpa sat in the living room every day, and often he stayed there through the night. Mom and I would sleep on the couch in the living room to be near him and keep vigil in case he needed anything during the night. During the day, while Mom ran errands with Grandma, I would stay with Grandpa, usually sitting on his lap. He had skinny legs, and he was constantly adjusting them so I wouldn't fall through to the floor. He loved me a lot. I loved him, too. Sometimes a nurse from hospice would come to give Grandpa a bath or just check on him. Soon he was staying in a unique bed in the guest bedroom. I stayed right beside Grandpa on the special bed to guard and protect him. Even while the nurse

tended to him, my protective instincts were in full operation.

Grandpa appreciated my being there with him. I knew he needed me. He was very sick. Everyone knew it, even me, so I refused to leave his bedside except to go outside and do business. One time, and the only time I think, I decided to stay with him instead of eating food. Something told me I shouldn't leave.

Sometimes he would reach out and touch me even though he didn't talk anymore. He didn't have to say anything. I just knew what I had to do. I stayed with him right until the end, and I never left his side until he drew his last breath, which was followed by a deep shudder as he exhaled for the last time.

Immediately after my dad died, there were a few last-minute details that needed attention. I drove my mother to Layton's Funeral Home. It was the only funeral home in my small hometown, and I felt at peace knowing my childhood friend George Layton would be taking care of my father and all the arrangements. I left Ernie home with the doggies while we tended to this very personal task.

When Mom took Grandma to Layton's, Daddy stayed at the house with Scooty and me. Cousin Karl came over to talk to Daddy and keep him company. They fixed a few things around the house that needed repair.

Then I heard Daddy ask Karl, "Have you seen Cray-Kur and Scooty?"

"No. I heard them bark when I first arrived, but I haven't seen them since."

"I'd better find them."

I could hear Daddy walking all over the house, but Karl and Daddy couldn't find Scooty and me. We could hear them calling for us everywhere. "Crazy Bones! Scooty!"

But we didn't answer. We stayed right where we were, huddled together with Grandma's cats, Lucy and Ethel, under the bed where Grandpa had died the day before.

Finally, Daddy found us. "What are you guys doing under the bed?"

There are things we animals know that humans just don't understand. We all wanted to be together in the room where Grandpa had been. His spirit was still there, and he loved all of us. It was a sad time. We all missed him. That was probably the only time in my life when I tolerated the company of felines, but they had the same senses Scooty and I did. Don't try to understand it. You just can't unless you are one of us.

Chapter 9

A Ride-in-the-Car

Ernie and I got married in a small ceremony near Long Sands Beach, where Cray-Kur and I ran. Neither of us ever believed in love at first sight until we met each other. We had known from the start we were destined to be together, so once we became an official family, it was time for Cray-Kur and me to pack and move to Virginia to be with Ernie and Scooty.

It didn't take long to sell my art supply business. My friend Lynn offered to buy it, and I knew she would do a great job running this business I had started many years ago. Everything else happened just as quickly. It was sad to sell my special home because it had become *our* home. The mail was forwarded, everything was packed for the movers, and goodbyes were said to my group of friends, a caring and dedicated support network. That was the hardest part. I had lived there longer than I had lived anywhere else, and I hadn't realized how deeply my roots had set until it was time to move. But a new adventure was ahead.

Crazy Bones sensed change and excitement. She was great at sensing all kinds of things. She was my little wonder dog. I traded in the Volvo for a small SUV for us. I liked it because Cray-Kur's crate fit in the front.

All details were checked off the to-do list, and the movers loaded the van. I crammed the SUV full of essentials, loaded Cray-Kur in her crate in the front seat so I could talk to her face-to-face during the trip, and off we went.

This ride-in-the-car is different. I like being in the front. I can see more. Hey, where are we going this time?

We drove down the lane and said goodbye to Uncle Roland, who was getting on in years and not in particularly good health. Sadly, we didn't realize it would be the last time we'd see him. We drove through town giving the last few goodbye hugs, and off we went. I'd miss living here, and I'd miss all my friends, but it was time to start a new chapter and head south of the Mason-Dixon Line and to our new home with Ernie and Scooty.

On the way to Virginia, we spent a few days and nights with my mother. Just before we arrived, I mentioned to Cray-Kur that we'd be seeing Grandma.

Thump-thump-thump-thump. Cray-Kur loved my family.

When we arrived, my mother was so delighted to see us. I could tell she missed my father, so we provided a welcome distraction for her. My parents had spent a lifetime together, and all of us felt the giant crater of emptiness my father's absence had created.

Cray-Kur and I visited family and friends during our short stay in New Jersey before we began the drive to Virginia.

Cousins Carol and Karl came over for dinner. They're cool! We also hung out with Uncle Lee and Uncle Jim, who referred to Scooty as "the bearded lady." Whatever! And soon we were off

for another ride-in-the-car and heading south to be with Daddy and the bearded lady!

Thump-thump-thump-thump.

We were on our way to our new home in Falls Church, Virginia, not far at all from the Potomac River, which separated Virginia from Washington, DC. The moving van had delivered thirty boxes of clothes, books, and whatever else I had packed. Ernie had stacked them in the dining room, and it was obvious what I would be doing for a few days upon my arrival. Ernie had a townhouse, which was a new kind of community for me. I was used to lots of space around me. There were a lot of adjustments to be made.

Why do you people need so many things? All you really need is food, clean water, and a comfortable bed.

Where on earth would I put everything? Unpacking wasn't fun, and when I needed a break, Cray-Kur and I explored the area for new places to run.

Now we were in suburbia. There were no pine forests, frozen lakes, or sandy beaches to run on. We had to obey traffic lights and use crosswalks. Crosswalks? I had to get in the habit of locking the house and car, because I hadn't done that in Maine or New Hampshire. This move was an enormous adjustment for both of us. When we ran, Cray-Kur's leash had to be kept short because of the proximity to cars. And many other people shared the sidewalks.

"This sure is different," I said wistfully to Cray-Kur as we ran one morning. "I need to find a route where I don't have to pay so much attention to, well, everything and everyone. I need to find a place where you can run freely, or at least with a longer lead."

Not exactly sure what you're saying here, Mom, but I get it. Where did all these people and cars come from? Why aren't they like Uncle Roland and all our other friends? People sure aren't very friendly here. And where are the woods where I can run without having to be on a leash? This place is weird.

Unfortunately, finding better places to run was a challenge, so we learned to adapt and run through neighborhoods that seemed less populated. We got to know only a few neighbors by name as we settled into our new life.

For a week or so, I opened box after box and found places to stash the pieces of my life. Thank goodness Ernie had an attic! I wished I had made larger donations to Goodwill before having *everything* shipped. Oh well. Too late.

Those first few months in northern Virginia passed quickly, and I learned how to get where I needed to go. Metro DC is a huge area, and I discovered I really didn't like driving on any road that ended in five: 495, 95, or 395. Cray-Kur was with me on some of these trips, and she could sense my anxiety. I hadn't seen her in distressed situations, but I could tell from her panting that she was also uncomfortable.

I took back roads whenever possible, but there weren't many of them, so I usually had to drive on those "five" roads.

I hadn't realized how close I really was to the United States Capitol until I drove right by it. I was awed at the sight. It was *right there!* The same thing with the Pentagon. These places were *real!* And they were so close, as were Arlington National Cemetery and all the memorials. I had to admit that Washington was very pretty at night and during the day when the cherry blossoms were in bloom.

I learned where *not* to go in DC. The first time I drove out of the parking garage at Union Station, I found that the exit to the street was on a different side of the building from the entrance. I had to decide whether to turn left or right. I had no clue where I was, so I turned right. *Wrong!* In two blocks, I was in a neighborhood with boarded-up buildings and where mattresses were hanging out ground-floor windows. It looked like a place where bad things happened. I felt my heart beat faster. I really didn't want to be here.

Okay, stay calm and keep the windows up and the doors locked. Make two right turns, roll through stop signs, and go somewhere—anywhere—just go! Just keep driving.

I felt so relieved I had my Crazy Bones with me for company. She was always such great support.

I never really felt at home in this part of Virginia. I missed my friends in New England, the clean air there, and the sense of safety. I was used to leaving my car unlocked with the keys in it. I wasn't used to so many people living close to each other, and some of our neighbors were less approachable than others.

It turned out that one of our neighbors was a spy. At least that was what other neighbors had said. Maybe they were trying to scare me. Well, it worked.

We lived in a nice development, but there were shootings every night just twenty miles away in downtown DC. I'd been a real country girl, but here I was, and here I'd stay until we retired to Florida. I had my husband, my health, and two wonderful dogs. I'd get by. It certainly wasn't the worst place in the world. Just different.

I enjoyed it when friends from New England would visit us because it relieved my homesickness. One of them was Robin, a friend from Maine, who traveled to DC a lot for business. We'd have great wine and pizza when she came to town. Cousin Carol often visited DC for business as well, and we'd enjoy the time together by exploring areas far from the city. Robin and Carol loved Cray-Kur and Scooty and always brought them treats.

Most people around us seemed so busy and not terribly interested in getting to know us except for Anna, who lived just up the street. She put treats on her front porch for dogs in the neighborhood. She worked from home, and she was very fond of Cray-Kur and Scooty. If I saw Anna gardening, I'd say, "Let's go see Anna."

Hey, Auntie Anna! How ya doin'? Got any more treats?

Thump-thump-thump-thump.

I was never sure who loved seeing the other more, Cray-Kur or Anna. Anna was a very special friend to Cray-Kur, Scooty, and me.

Ernie's friends, Greg and Cheryl, became my friends, and Cray-Kur took an immediate liking to both of them. They were dog people. When I'd mention that we were going to Greg and Cheryl's house or that they were coming for dinner, Little Miss Waggy Tail would show her excitement.

Thump-thump-thump-thump.

I adjusted once again. Wherever I am, I'm fine, as long as Mom is there. I've moved a lot in my life, and I always made new friends. Mom says I'm just a person in doggy clothes. Uncle Greg and Auntie Cheryl had a dog, Lickey, who had gone blind. I felt sorry for Lickey, so

whenever we were together, I led him around because he had trouble finding his own way.

Uncle Greg and Auntie Cheryl had a house on a lake, and sometimes we went there on weekends in the summer. It was a nice getaway for all of us. Mom and I could run on the road around the lake. That was nice because there weren't many cars. Daddy could go fishing with Uncle Greg and Auntie Cheryl while Scooty and Lickey could lounge. It's what they did best.

Sometimes I'd watch Mom and Dad go out on a Jet Ski while I stayed on the dock with Scooty and Lickey. Other times we would all go out on a big pontoon boat, except for Lickey. He just stayed at home where it was safer. Mom, Dad, Uncle Greg, and Auntie Cheryl would sometimes jump off the boat and swim around to cool off. Mom took me in the water with her once. I'm a good swimmer, and I liked the lake, but I didn't like going off the boat. Looking up at the boat from down in the water scared me. The ladder was beyond my reach. So I stayed with Mom and swam beside her as we circled the boat. Once around the boat was plenty. Mom could tell I was getting tired, so she lifted me onto a platform, and then she climbed a ladder to get me back in the boat. It was refreshing to go in the water though, and Mom dried me with a towel. She knew that felt good. She knows me so well.

One morning at the lake house, Mom decided to go kayaking. Scooty stayed in bed with Daddy. The lake was very still early in the morning because the power boaters and water-skiers hadn't gotten up yet. Uncle Greg was an early riser like Mom and me, so when he saw us heading toward the water, he joined us.

"Need a hand?" he called.

"I think I do," Mom answered, as she realized the kayak could tip over very easily. With his help, she got seated in the kayak, and then Uncle Greg picked me up and gently handed me to her. They both moved very slowly so the kayak wouldn't tip over.

I stood with my hind paws on Mom's seat and my front paws on the top of the kayak for balance. This was great, but Mom kept telling me not to move. I guess her balance wasn't as good as mine.

Gently and silently, Mom paddled out into the lake. A paddle stroke on the left, a paddle stroke on the right. A paddle stroke on the left, a paddle stroke on the right. She had gotten the hang of it! We explored a cove and waved to a man fishing off his dock. He was smiling. Maybe he had never seen a dog kayaking before. My tail was wagging because it was such fun, but Mom kept telling me to be still. What was up with that?

When Mom got tired, she paddled back to the lake house, where Uncle Greg met us near the dock. He waded into the water and Mom paddled toward him. Uncle Greg reached in the kayak to lift me out. He knew just how to do it. I guess he has to lift Lickey a lot. He carried me to shore while Mom tied up the kayak. Dad and Auntie Cheryl had come down to the dock to greet us.

"Cray-Kur! Did you have fun? Did you like the kayak?" they called.

Well, yeah! Who wouldn't? I wanted to do that again! It was so much fun seeing new places with my mom! We both slept really well at the lake house.

Chapter 10

Life Changers

We had lived in Virginia about a year, and despite the fact I didn't enjoy living in a densely populated suburb of Washington, DC, it had become our home. We had carved out our routines, and both dogs knew the patterns and schedules of our days. They were so smart in their own ways. I already knew that Crazy Bones read people well, and Scooty also showed that same skill. That became very evident one day when Ernie came home from work early. The doggies knew something was up before I did. Ernie set his briefcase on the kitchen counter and smiled his usual smile, asking, "How are the doggies?" He was trying to act nonchalant. Crazy Bones and Scooter stood very still. They knew something was up.

Ernie knelt down, petted their heads, and rubbed their bellies as he did every night when he came home. But it wasn't long before I read his body language, too. Ernie was slouching, and his shoulders drooped.

"What's wrong? Do you feel okay? Did you have a bad day?" I asked, trying to be gentle but needing to know what on earth had made my husband look sick to his stomach. "Are you okay?" I could get pretty impatient when I suspected trouble.

Uh-oh. Something's not right.

Ernie sank uncharacteristically into his easy chair. The news was not good. His company had been sold to a larger one, and soon he would be out of a job. This had been in the works for months, but the reality of the decision was hard to take. It was the end of an era. It was an end to all Ernie had known and done all his life. He moved toward the kitchen deliberately and mechanically, the way someone in shock goes through the motions.

Ernie knew I would not be totally heartbroken over this news because I had been looking forward to the day when we could leave the Metro DC area. Don't get me wrong. Washington, DC, is an absolutely great place to visit, but dealing with the traffic and congestion every day made me long for the days of living in New England where life was better and the air was cleaner. I missed the slower pace, and I missed living where people seemed to take the time to enjoy what and who was around them. While I felt bad for Ernie, I couldn't wait to leave this place and move to the more relaxed lifestyle of southwest Florida, a move we'd been planning for our retirement.

I tried to temper Ernie's news. "Think of the bright side. We will be near the Gulf of Mexico. The dogs can run on the beach. We can spend more quality time together. Life will be simpler. I'd love that, and I think you would, too!"

"I know. I've been trying to see things that way, too. But there's so much I have to do before we can move. Besides, I do want to explore other job options here."

"No problem. We will do what we have to do. Most importantly, we have each other, and together, anything is possible." It had become our motto, and here was our chance to prove it to each other.

I always wanted Ernie to feel supported. If we did have to move, it wouldn't be for two or three months because attorneys for both sides of the transaction had to sort things out. Those months would give Ernie some time to look for another job, but it was a disappointing challenge. Although he was well-known and respected by his peers in the area, he was already at the top of his field and close to retirement age. The fact was a sore reminder that we were getting older and no one wanted to hire him. It was a sad time, and I really felt sorry for him.

We had to move and put our retirement plan into action a little sooner than we had expected. While I wasn't upset about leaving the area, Ernie had spent most of his life here, so the thought of relocating was more difficult for him. At least he had Crazy Bones, Scooty, and me to provide comfort, continuity, and wonderful distractions in the next phase of our lives. We'd manage.

We got rid of stuff we didn't use or need, and then signed a contract with a moving company. Whatever was left would soon be in boxes, and our cars would be packed with only the essential items we'd need for a week. Driving from Virginia to southwest Florida was a trip we'd already made several times as we scouted out retirement living options. I actually enjoy driving, and of course, a ride-in-the-car was always great fun for Crazy Bones. I knew I was fortunate to have a dog who enjoyed road trips as much as I did.

I found a box I had packed the day before labeled Art Supplies. I needed something to do, so I opened it and pulled out a small canvas I'd been working on. Now would be a good time to finish it. I dug out my palette, mixed some acrylics, and slipped into what Ernie called "my zone." It would be a good time to reflect and concentrate on colors and light, so when the doorbell rang, I jumped.

Are you kidding? A bold streak of gray paint was an unwelcome addition to the middle of my canvas. Annoyed, I set down my brush and opened the door.

"Here you go," announced the strong, familiar voice of Frank, our mail carrier.

"How are you today, Miss Elizabeth? I need your signature right here."

A package from my sister had arrived. She, too, was moving due to a job relocation and wanted to get rid of some treasures. She had thought I might like a particular antique piece from our family's farm. I appreciated the thought, but our move was only days away, and I didn't relish the thought of packing one more breakable heirloom.

Frank handed me the rest of the mail and wished me a good afternoon. I was distracted by the fragile package and nearly overlooked a letter forwarded from New England. *Oh my!* I recognized the handwriting. It was a letter from Charles! He *had* written back. My heart started pounding. This could be the moment of truth. Could I handle it?

I decided to wait before opening the letter to get myself completely settled and psychologically prepared for whatever was in the letter. I put the letter on the kitchen counter, heated water for tea, then took Scooty and Crazy Bones for a quick walk while the tea steeped. With a cleared space at the kitchen table, I sat down with my tea. Carefully and methodically, I unsealed the envelope, pulled out the neatly folded letter, and opened it with nervous anticipation. I began to read.

Dear Miss Elizabeth,

Thank you very much for sending the photographs. That was my dog. She looks as sweet and mischievous as ever. I like the collar she is wearing. I can tell you take good care of her.

I was the only owner Jersey ever had. We got her when she was six weeks old, and she lived with us until she got left behind when Katrina struck. We had no choice. Our home was flooded, and we had to evacuate. They wouldn't let us take Jersey in the rescue boat, and that was it. We never saw her again. We worried about her and prayed she'd be okay. It was almost two weeks before we could even begin to try and find her. By that time, she had probably already been sent to a shelter.

We were bused to a small town near Knoxville and rebuilt our lives. Knoxville has a great university with plenty of things to keep us busy and entertained. My kids are both students at UT, my wife works there, and the people are kind. Things have a way of working out. We are all so relieved and grateful that Jersey was saved and that she now lives with someone who takes good care of her. Thanks again for writing. If you're ever near Knoxville, look us up! Take care of that special dog of yours.

God bless you.

Charles de LaSepps

I couldn't believe it. I had found Cray-Kur's first owner, and he sounded like a very nice person. I'd pieced together Cray-Kur's life! But the tsunami of relief that washed over me was because Charles wasn't asking for his dog back. Charles's words, *"Take care of that special dog of yours,"* made me cry for joy.

I grabbed the phone and plopped down on the sofa. I could barely dial Ernie's cell.

"Hi, honey! This is a nice surprise! How are you?"

"I couldn't wait until you got home. I had to call you now."

"What's wrong? Are you okay? Is everything all right?"

Obviously, the tone of my voice was alarming. How could it not be? This was *huge!* I couldn't wait a minute, let alone two hours, for him to come home and tell him my news.

"Sorry, no. I mean, yes. Yes, everything is okay. Remember that guy, Charles, I told you about? He was the owner of Cray-Kur before Katrina. Remember?"

Charles? Charles? I know that name. Why is Mom getting so excited? What's going on?

"He identified Cray-Kur from my photos. I tracked down her original owner! Can you believe it?"

"Okay, slow down. I am happy for you, but does he want her back?" Ernie was naturally wary of people he hadn't met.

"No. He said he was happy I'd made contact with him." Details spewed out of my mouth faster than Ernie could make sense of them, so we decided to continue the conversation when he got home.

I drafted a short note to thank Charles for getting back to me.

Dear Charles,

Since my last letter to you, I moved to northern Virginia, just outside DC. But we aren't here for long. We are relocating to southwest Florida next month.

If you'd ever like to see Jersey/Cray-Kur, or if you're ever in Florida, please let me know.

Thanks so much for helping me solve the puzzle of Cray-Kur's past. Let's stay in touch. Kind regards to your family. Enjoy Knoxville!

Elizabeth

My head was spinning. While I still didn't really know too much about Cray-Kur's past, I felt relieved to know she'd been in a good home. Her history was less of a mystery, and I'd come full circle on my mission to contact her original owner.

I collapsed on the couch next to Scooty and reached down to stroke the head of my little Crazy Bones, who had followed me into the living room. "I love you, Crazy Bones."

What's not to love?

Thump-thump-thump-thump.

Cray-Kur jumped up to be next to me, and Scooty shifted to make room for her sister. I lay still for a very long time holding both doggies while trying to imagine what Charles and his family had gone through— losing their home, losing their dog, losing everything. I don't think I could ever really understand what they went through without having gone through it myself. It must have been devastating.

I am blessed. Yes, there have been a few hills and valleys in my life, but really nothing at all compared to what Charles and thousands of others had been through. And to think I had acquired this amazing little doggy as a direct result of Charles's misfortune. I looked at Crazy Bones, this special bundle of energy who ran like the dickens, leaped over mountains of snow, and served as my protector doggy. She was watching me. I closed my eyes and felt a tear run down my face, but Crazy Bones quickly licked that tear off. I smiled.

Chapter 11

A Long Ride-in-the-Car

The movers loaded our life into a big truck. It was a little unsettling, as moving always is. But this time I knew what was ahead and happily looked forward to it. Ernie had bought a place for us and assured me I'd love it. I trusted him. The energy level around us was palpable.

What's going on? We just moved here. Why are these men taking away all our things? Why does Mom keep talking about a ride-in-the-car? We usually didn't go through all this just for a ride-in-the-car.

Scooty was anxious with the invasion of strangers in our home, and Daddy tried to

soothe her, but she became a nervous wreck! So Daddy took her for a long walk. We both knew something was up, but I didn't fuss. I just let Mom put me in my crate and let Daddy try to calm Scooty. Thank goodness he put Scooty in *his* car! She was driving me nuts.

Mom and Dad hugged each other, then got in their own cars and started to drive. We drove. And drove. And drove.

Then we would stop, and every time we stopped, there was Daddy with Scooty in the car next to us!

Thump-thump-thump-thump.

How did you do that? I asked Daddy. He would smile and kiss the top of my head. His answer was simply, "Crazy Bones! There you are, Waggy Tail!"

Whatever.

That's what we did for three days. Driving, stopping to relieve ourselves, having some food, then driving some more. This was a *really* long ride-in-the-car. We spent a couple of nights in hotels, but Scooty and I couldn't explore any new places because we were right back in the car and on the road again. And again. Driving, driving, driving. I couldn't wait to get to wherever we were going!

At one rest stop, Daddy explained to Scooty and me that we were in Florida, and we'd be living here for the rest of our lives. No more moving.

Scooty, this is a good thing. Trust me.

In a matter of hours, we arrived at our destination. I knew a place just like this where we ran on the beach off leash. I couldn't wait to tell Scooty about running on a beach.

Mom and Dad didn't seem too excited, but I think they were tired from driving. Once they unloaded the cars, they poured some cold water into bowls for us and ice water into glasses for themselves. I guess it was too hard for them to drink out of our water bowls. Mom and Dad started to relax. In fact, after dinner and a long walk on the beach, we all felt much better.

I explained to Crazy Bones that we would live here on Sanibel Island. No more moving. We could run on the beach, find exotic seashells, and enjoy life together.

Cool! I thought. Mom sounded happy and content, and if Mom was content, I was content.

We found a large piece of driftwood near the dunes, and Mom sat down. I sat at her feet in the cool sand. Together we watched Daddy and Scooty walk up the beach toward us.

Swish-swish-swish-swish went my waggy tail, creating a design in the sand much like the pattern that wipers make on the car's windshield when it rains.

Without a word, Daddy sat down next to Mom, and Scooty sat next to me, her stub of a tail wagging a hundred miles an hour. She, too, was accumulating nicknames. First the Bearded Lady. Now Waggy Stub.

Beachcombers walked by, but their focus was on the Gulf and the unusual purple-and-orange colors of the late afternoon sun reflecting off the waves and the wet sand.

Mom and Daddy sat close together and stroked us. The sun was setting, and it cast a beautiful, warm glow on everything. It was quiet except for the gentle sound of the waves of the gulf gently rushing up the beach, then down again over the shells and pebbles at the edge of the water. Occasionally, people said hi, but most people just stopped and watched the sunset. It was serene.

Although this is a new beginning, I feel like I've been here before. The smells and sounds . . . there is something about the water here that calms me. I don't know why, but it just seems so familiar. I smiled up at Mom, and she smiled back. I love it here! There have been a few traumas in my life, but now my life is wonderful! I have lots of friends and a mom who runs with me, plays with me, and loves me more than life itself. I'm glad I rescued her.

Swish-swish-swish-swish.

Chapter 12

Home on the Gulf of Mexico

Moving to Florida was much less traumatic than moving to Metro DC. It took no time at all to settle in. Ernie began working in a hardware store, and I volunteer at a wildlife conservation program. We live a simpler life in our small house. We sold most of our furnishings, and it was a refreshing change to downsize, keeping only the things we really wanted and needed.

We live a block from the beach, and our home is elevated on pilings for protection against flooding. We have an unobstructed view of the Gulf of Mexico. It is exhilarating to wake up to the sound and smell of the surf, and then at night to see all the stars against the dark sky. No city lights to ruin this view!

Our little home is convenient to everything, including shops that put out bowls of water for all the dogs that walk by. I love how people are so friendly here, friendly toward dogs and other people. Crazy Bones and Scooty like their new home, and they've made many friends in our small village. Everything has fallen into place, a place that feels so right.

Everybody knows my name, or at least one of my names. This place is awesome! Can we go for a walk? Run on the beach?

Thump-thump-thump-thump.

One evening, as we all sat on the beach watching the dolphins play in the Gulf, I had an overwhelming sense of peace and happiness that I had not experienced in a very long time. Here we were—our little family—in paradise. I looked down at Crazy Bones.

There are certain times when Mom looks at me in a special way, and this is one of those times. She says she loves me using only her eyes. I totally get her!

Swish-swish-swish-swish.

As for Crazy Bones, what a life she has had! She is home again on the Gulf of Mexico, not too far from where she spent the first part of her life with Charles and his family. The hair around Cray-Kur's mouth and on her paws has turned as gray as my hair, but she still has plenty of energy. We are both getting older. Crazy Bones has been such a trooper through all my moves and changes in my life.

Cray-Kur is mellow most of the time, but when the late afternoon thunderstorms roll in, she needs to be right next to me or on me. She trembles when the storms approach and jumps at the loud thunderclaps. Scooty, on the other hand, is uncharacteristically mellow and unfazed. Crazy Bones must associate those sounds with a horrible time in her life.

I am a better person for all the lessons I've learned from Crazy Bones. I've learned to loosen my grip on the steering wheel of life. I've learned what unconditional love means. And I've learned how to be content and enjoy life. She has taught me so much more than I have ever taught her.

I continue to wake up early, but not as early as before. We now get up when there's a faint

glow in the morning sky. Mom takes Scooty and me out to do our business. Instead of running, the three of us go for a long walk on the beach before returning home for breakfast. When we get home, Mom makes coffee, wakes up Daddy, and then feeds Scooty and me. It's pretty much the same every day, but it never gets boring.

When she isn't doing volunteer work, Mom paints in her studio and sells her art in local shops. Daddy works close to home, so we get to spend a lot of time playing together. Now and then we go for a ride-in-the-car, and every day we go for a walk through our little town and on the beach.

We've got lots of friends here, and they call out to us, "Hi, Scooty! Hi, Crazy Bones!"

Sometimes in the late afternoon when it isn't hot, Mom takes me for a run on the beach while Scooty stays with Daddy. It's better that way. Let me tell you, Scooty is a wild thing on the beach. She runs over to everybody to say hi. I just mind my own business. Mom would rather run with me than chase Scooty.

We get bad thunderstorms here. They never used to bother me when Mom and I lived in other places, but they are so loud here, and they remind me of sounds from a long time ago. I don't like them, so I snuggle up close to Mom. She understands. But I love being by the water. It is familiar and comforting.

As a loyal and faithful companion, I take care of Mom. Almost everywhere she goes, I'm with her. We were meant to be together.

I am a good sister to Scooty, but there is so much more to teach her! Daddy loves Scooty almost as much as he loves me. I have a great life, and I've got a mom who is crazy about me.

Thump-thump-thump-thump.

Scooty

Crazy Bones

The End

Author's Note about Hurricane Katrina

Hurricane Katrina made landfall on the Gulf Coast of the United States as a Category 3 hurricane on August 29, 2005. The intensity of the storm grew to a Category 5, and it became one of the most devastating hurricanes on record. Hurricane Katrina ravaged the city of New Orleans for three full days, causing levees to break as a massive storm surge brought ten to twenty-eight feet of floodwater into the coastal region. Estimates exceeded $100 billion in damage and claimed more than eighteen hundred lives, making it the "single most catastrophic natural disaster in US history," according to the Federal Emergency Management Agency (FEMA).

Evacuation efforts focused on rescuing human lives, but an estimated 250,000 animals were left behind to fend for themselves. Many of them perished. Animal rescue efforts began as an ad hoc group of volunteers, and soon the group named themselves Animal Rescue New Orleans (ARNO) and set up makeshift centers. Volunteers searched abandoned homes, scrambled to rooftops to rescue stranded animals, and risked their lives combing through partially dilapidated buildings in search of survivors. Volunteer drivers from around the country worked in relay teams to transport pets to new homes in other parts of the US. They saved more than 15,000 pets, but an estimated 150,000 died.

As a result of the animal death toll following Hurricane Katrina, Governor Kathleen Blanco signed the Louisiana Pet Evacuation bill into effect. It required the rescue of pets to be part of evacuation efforts. The federal government followed suit and passed the Pets Evacuation and Transportation Standards (PETS) Act, which mandated that pets had to be evacuated with their owners. These two pieces of legislation finally recognized the important roles pets have in many households and lives.

Research in pediatric medicine, family medicine, mental health, and psychology around the world has shown that there are significant benefits to having a pet and that the human-animal bond can be used to improve people's lives. Health professionals use trained animals in a variety of ways from seeing-eye dogs that assist the visually impaired to dogs trained to detect seizures to easing loneliness in elderly and disenfranchised populations. Animals can also be used in occupational, speech therapy, and physical therapy. According to the National Center for Health Research, a study on *The Benefits of Pets for Human Health* conducted by Dana Casciotti, PhD and Diana Zuckerman, PhD published in NCHR's The Voice for Prevention, Treatment, and Policy in Washington, DC found that heart health, blood pressure, and mood improved among people who had companion animals. They also found that children's anxiety and behavioral disorders may also be reduced with companion animals, and depression in adults and children is reduced when they spend time with companion pets.

The influential role of pets in society is important and noteworthy, and providing support for their care and welfare is imperative and commands our ongoing consideration.

About the Authors

Dr. Lynne Wissink-Tressler is an animal lover who supports local animal shelters and rescue efforts. She has traveled extensively while pursuing her educational ambitions and is passionate about writing, teaching, and sharing stories about the dog she rescued. She resides near the Gulf Coast of Florida.

Crazy Bones is also well traveled, having started her life in or near New Orleans. Following Hurricane Katrina, she was abandoned and sent to a shelter. She made her way to northern New England in hopes of being adopted. She enjoys running on the beaches of Sanibel and Captiva Islands and sharing stories about the woman she rescued.

We hope you have enjoyed Lynne Wissink-Tressler's wonderful story of *CRAZY BONES: The Tale of a Waggy Tail.*

Please check out the other books offered on our website at www.bluewaterpress.com.